The Quote Book on Success to Sound Smart at Work and Home.

Jack Dhade

The Quote Book on Success to Sound Smart at Work
and Home

Published by Independent

Texas, USA

ISBN: 9798333519030

Printed in USA

Dedication

"To all those who strive for greatness,

This book is dedicated to the dreamers, the doers, the relentless pursuers of success. To those who wake up each day with a fire in their heart and a vision in their mind, refusing to settle for anything less than extraordinary.

May you always find the courage to take risks, the resilience to overcome failures, and the wisdom to learn from every experience. Let your journey be fueled by passion, guided by determination, and illuminated by the belief that you are capable of achieving greatness.

Here's to your relentless pursuit of success. May you continue to rise, inspire, and leave an indelible mark on the world."

With unwavering admiration,

Jack Dhade

Table of Contents

Introduction: The Essence of Success and the Divide from Failure

Success, a concept revered and pursued across cultures and generations, represents more than just the attainment of goals or the accumulation of wealth. It embodies a state of fulfillment, the realization of one's potential, and the manifestation of dreams into reality. The path to success is often meandering and fraught with obstacles, yet it is the journey itself that molds individuals into their most accomplished selves.

The Nature of Success

At its core, success is subjective. It varies from person to person, influenced by personal values, ambitions, and life circumstances. For some, success may mean achieving professional acclaim, while for others, it might signify creating a loving family or contributing to the betterment of society. Despite these differences, common threads weave through the fabric of success:

Vision and Goals

Success begins with a clear vision and well-defined goals. This vision acts as a guiding star, directing efforts and keeping one focused amidst distractions.

Persistence and Resilience

The journey to success is seldom smooth. It demands persistence and the ability to bounce back from failures. Resilience transforms setbacks into learning opportunities, fueling the drive to continue.

Hard Work and Dedication

Success requires consistent effort and dedication. It is the result of small, cumulative actions taken over time rather than a single monumental effort.

Adaptability and Innovation

The world is ever-changing, and so are the paths to success. The ability to adapt and innovate in response to new challenges and opportunities is crucial.

Positive Mindset

A positive, growth-oriented mindset helps individuals see possibilities where others see obstacles. It fosters optimism, creativity, and a willingness to take risks.

The Divide from Failure

The thin line separating success from failure is often defined by how one navigates the journey. While success and failure are two sides of the same coin, the distinguishing factors lie in the mindset and actions of the individual.

Perspective on Failure

Successful people view failure as a stepping stone rather than a roadblock. They learn from their mistakes, refine their strategies, and persist with renewed vigor. Failure is seen as an integral part of the growth process.

Consistency vs. Complacency

Success demands consistent effort. Those who succeed maintain a steady pace, continuously working towards their goals. In contrast, failure often results from complacency or giving up too soon.

Proactive Attitude

Successful individuals take proactive steps towards their goals. They plan, execute, and adjust their actions as needed. In contrast, those who fail often remain passive, waiting for success to come to them.

Embracing Change

Success is linked to the ability to embrace change and adapt. Those who resist change and stick rigidly to outdated methods are more likely to encounter failure.

Support Systems

Building a strong support network of mentors, peers, and advisors can make a significant difference. Successful individuals seek guidance and collaborate, while those who fail often attempt to go it alone.

Conclusion

Success is not a destination but a journey marked by continuous effort, learning, and adaptation. It is a blend of vision, persistence, hard work, and a positive mindset. The divide between success and failure is nuanced, influenced by how one perceives and responds to challenges. By understanding these dynamics, one can navigate the path to success with greater clarity and purpose, turning aspirations into achievements.

Chapter 1: Famous Failures - The Stepping Stones to Success

The road to success is often paved with failures. History is replete with stories of individuals who faced significant setbacks and obstacles before achieving greatness. These tales of perseverance and resilience serve as powerful reminders that failure is not the end but a crucial part of the journey to success. In this chapter, we will explore the stories of famous failures and how they overcame their challenges to leave an indelible mark on the world.

Thomas Edison: The Inventor Who Never Gave Up

Thomas Edison, one of the greatest inventors in history, is a prime example of turning failure into success. Edison's journey was fraught with countless experiments that didn't yield the desired results. His most famous invention, the incandescent light bulb, took over 1,000 attempts to perfect. When questioned about his failures, Edison famously replied, "I have not failed. I've just found 10,000 ways that won't work." His relentless perseverance and unwavering belief in his vision ultimately led to groundbreaking innovations that transformed the modern world.

J.K. Rowling: From Rejection to Literary Fame

Before becoming one of the most successful authors of all time, J.K. Rowling faced numerous rejections and hardships. Struggling as a single mother living on welfare, she found solace in writing. Her manuscript for "Harry Potter and the Philosopher's Stone" was rejected by twelve major publishing houses before Bloomsbury finally accepted it. Today, the Harry Potter series is a global phenomenon, proving that perseverance in the face of rejection can lead to extraordinary success.

Walt Disney: Fired for Lack of Imagination

Walt Disney, the visionary behind the beloved Disney empire, was once fired from a newspaper job for "lacking imagination and having no good ideas." Undeterred, Disney continued to pursue his passion for animation and storytelling. He faced numerous financial setbacks and business failures, including a bankrupt animation studio. However, his resilience and creativity eventually led to the creation of Mickey Mouse and the foundation of a company that has brought joy to millions worldwide.

Steve Jobs: A Visionary's Comeback

Steve Jobs, the co-founder of Apple Inc., experienced a dramatic career setback when he was ousted from his own company in 1985. Instead of giving up, Jobs used this failure as an opportunity to innovate and create. He founded NeXT, a computer platform development company, and acquired Pixar, a struggling animation studio. Both ventures proved successful, and Jobs' return to Apple in 1997 marked the beginning of a remarkable turnaround, leading to the development of iconic products like the iPod, iPhone, and iPad. Jobs' story is a testament to the power of resilience and the importance of embracing failure as a catalyst for future success.

Oprah Winfrey: Rising Above Adversity

Oprah Winfrey's journey to becoming a media mogul and philanthropist was fraught with personal and professional challenges. Born into poverty and experiencing a troubled childhood, Winfrey faced numerous obstacles on her path to success. Early in her career, she was demoted from her job as a news anchor because she was deemed "unfit for television." However, her authenticity and talent shone through when she transitioned to hosting her own talk show. "The Oprah Winfrey Show" became a cultural phenomenon, and Winfrey's story of overcoming adversity continues to inspire millions around the world.

Albert Einstein: The Late Bloomer

Albert Einstein, one of the most renowned physicists in history, faced early academic challenges. He did not speak fluently until the age of nine and struggled in school, leading some teachers to believe he was intellectually disabled. Despite these setbacks, Einstein's curiosity and passion for science never wavered. His groundbreaking theories, including the theory of relativity, revolutionized the field of physics and earned him the Nobel Prize in 1921. Einstein's story illustrates that early failures do not determine one's potential for future success.

Michael Jordan: The Missed Shots

Michael Jordan, widely regarded as one of the greatest basketball players of all time, faced numerous failures throughout his career. He was cut from his high school varsity basketball team, which could have discouraged him from pursuing the sport. Instead, Jordan used this setback as motivation to improve his skills and work harder. His determination paid off, leading to an illustrious career with six NBA championships and numerous accolades. Jordan's famous quote, "I've missed more than 9,000 shots in my career. I've lost almost 300 games. Twenty-six times, I've been trusted to take the game-winning shot and missed. I've failed over and over and over again in my life. And that is why I succeed," encapsulates his belief in the power of persistence.

Henry Ford: Learning from Bankruptcy

Henry Ford, the founder of Ford Motor Company, faced significant financial difficulties before revolutionizing the automotive industry. His early ventures, including the Detroit Automobile Company, ended in bankruptcy. However, Ford's innovative vision and determination led to the creation of the Model T and the implementation of the assembly line, which transformed manufacturing processes and made cars affordable for the masses. Ford's ability to learn from his failures and continue pursuing his vision ultimately reshaped transportation and industrial production.

Vincent Van Gogh: A Legacy Beyond His Lifetime

Vincent Van Gogh, now celebrated as one of the greatest painters in history, struggled with mental illness and poverty throughout his life. During his lifetime, he sold only a few paintings and was often dismissed by critics. Despite these challenges, Van Gogh continued to paint with passion and dedication, producing over 2,000 artworks. His work gained recognition posthumously, and he is now revered for his contributions to art. Van Gogh's story underscores the importance of staying true to one's passion, regardless of external validation.

Conclusion: Embracing Failure as a Stepping Stone

The stories of these famous failures highlight a common theme: the road to success is rarely straightforward. Each of these individuals faced significant obstacles and setbacks but ultimately achieved greatness through perseverance, resilience, and an unwavering belief in their vision. Their experiences remind us that failure is not a final destination but a stepping stone on the path to success. By embracing failure, learning from it, and continuing to strive for our goals, we can turn setbacks into opportunities for growth and achievement.

Chapter 2: Typical Indicators of Success

Success is a multifaceted concept that can be measured in various ways. While the definition of success can vary greatly depending on individual goals and values, there are common indicators that often signify success in both personal and professional realms. These indicators serve as benchmarks that help individuals gauge their progress and achievements. In this chapter, we will explore the typical indicators of success and how they manifest in different aspects of life.

Professional Indicators of Success

Career Advancement

Promotions and Raises: Climbing the corporate ladder through promotions and receiving salary raises are clear indicators of professional success. These milestones reflect recognition of an individual's skills, dedication, and contributions to their organization.

Leadership Roles: Attaining leadership positions, such as becoming a manager, director, or executive, signifies trust and respect within a company. Leadership roles often come with increased responsibilities and influence.

Financial Stability

Increased Earnings: A steady increase in income over time indicates financial growth and stability. This financial success allows individuals to afford a comfortable lifestyle and invest in their future.

Savings and Investments: Building a robust savings account, investing in stocks, real estate, or other assets, and planning for retirement are important financial indicators of success.

Professional Recognition

Awards and Honors: Receiving industry awards, honors, or accolades demonstrates a high level of expertise and accomplishment in one's field.

Publications and Patents: Publishing research papers, articles, or books, as well as obtaining patents for innovative ideas, are indicators of professional achievement and intellectual contribution.

Job Satisfaction

Fulfillment and Passion: Finding joy and passion in one's work is a critical indicator of success. Job satisfaction often leads to higher productivity and overall well-being.

 Work-Life Balance: Successfully balancing professional responsibilities with personal life is an important aspect of career success. Achieving this balance contributes to long-term happiness and sustainability.

Personal Indicators of Success

Healthy Relationships

Strong Family Bonds: Maintaining close and supportive relationships with family members is a key indicator of personal success. Family provides emotional support and a sense of belonging.

Meaningful Friendships: Building and nurturing meaningful friendships that offer companionship, trust, and mutual respect is another sign of personal success.

Personal Growth and Development

Continuous Learning: Engaging in lifelong learning through education, self-improvement, and acquiring new skills reflects a commitment to personal growth.

Hobbies and Interests: Pursuing hobbies and interests outside of work adds richness to life and contributes to a well-rounded sense of fulfillment.

Physical and Mental Health

Healthy Lifestyle: Prioritizing physical health through regular exercise, a balanced diet, and adequate rest is a vital indicator of personal success.

Mental Well-Being: Maintaining mental health through stress management, mindfulness, and seeking professional help when needed reflects a balanced and healthy life.

Sense of Purpose

Achieving Personal Goals: Setting and achieving personal goals, whether they are related to career, family, or personal interests, is a strong indicator of success.

Contribution to Society: Volunteering, philanthropy, and contributing to the community or society at large reflect a broader sense of purpose and success beyond personal gains.

Indicators of Success in Business

Profitability

Revenue Growth: Consistent increase in revenue and profits indicates a successful business. It shows the ability to generate income and sustain operations over time.

Cost Management: Effective management of costs and expenses while maximizing profitability is a crucial business success indicator.

Market Share

Customer Base Expansion: Growing the customer base and capturing a larger market share reflect business success and competitiveness.

Brand Recognition: Building a strong brand that is recognized and respected in the market is a significant indicator of business success.

Innovation and Adaptability

Product Development: Continuously developing new products or services that meet market needs and preferences is a hallmark of a successful business.

Adaptability to Change: Successfully navigating market changes, economic fluctuations, and industry trends shows resilience and adaptability.

Customer Satisfaction

Positive Feedback: Receiving positive customer reviews, testimonials, and high satisfaction ratings are indicators of a successful business.

Customer Loyalty: Building a loyal customer base that returns for repeat business and refers others is a key measure of success.

Conclusion: Measuring Success

Success is a dynamic and evolving concept, influenced by personal aspirations, professional goals, and societal standards. The typical indicators of success outlined in this chapter provide a framework for understanding and measuring achievements in various aspects of life. Whether in the realm of career, personal development, or business, these indicators serve as benchmarks that help individuals and organizations assess their progress and set new goals. By recognizing and celebrating these indicators, one can gain a deeper appreciation of the journey and the milestones that define success.

Chapter 3: The Pathways to Achievement - How Famous People Reached Their Goals

Achieving one's goals often requires a blend of vision, determination, hard work, and resilience. Throughout history, many famous individuals have exemplified these qualities, overcoming obstacles and setbacks to reach remarkable levels of success. In this chapter, we will delve into the journeys of several well-known figures, exploring how they achieved their goals and the lessons we can learn from their experiences.

Elon Musk: The Visionary Innovator

Elon Musk, the founder of SpaceX and Tesla, is a prime example of a visionary who has achieved extraordinary goals through relentless pursuit and innovation. Musk's journey began with a deep fascination for technology and space. Despite facing significant financial and technical challenges, Musk's determination and willingness to take risks propelled him forward.

Early Career: Musk co-founded Zip2, an online city guide, which he sold for nearly $300 million. He then co-founded X.com, which later became PayPal and was acquired by eBay for $1.5 billion.

SpaceX: Musk founded SpaceX with the ambitious goal of making space travel affordable and eventually colonizing Mars. Despite early failures, including multiple rocket launch failures, SpaceX became the first privately funded company to send a spacecraft to the International Space Station.

Tesla: Musk's goal of accelerating the world's transition to sustainable energy led him to join Tesla Motors. Under his leadership, Tesla has revolutionized the electric car industry, overcoming production challenges and skeptics to become a leader in clean energy.

Lesson: Elon Musk's story highlights the importance of having a bold vision, embracing risk, and persisting through challenges to achieve groundbreaking success.

Oprah Winfrey: The Media Mogul

Oprah Winfrey's rise from poverty to becoming one of the most influential media personalities in the world is a testament to the power of resilience and self-belief. Winfrey's journey was marked by personal hardships, but her determination to overcome these challenges drove her to achieve her goals.

Early Life: Winfrey faced a difficult childhood, experiencing poverty and abuse. However, she excelled in school and earned a scholarship to Tennessee State University.

Career Breakthrough: Winfrey's first major break came when she was hired as a news anchor. Although she faced setbacks, including being demoted from her position, she eventually found her calling in talk shows.

The Oprah Winfrey Show: Winfrey's show became a cultural phenomenon, making her a household name. She used her platform to inspire and empower millions of people worldwide.

Philanthropy and Entrepreneurship: Beyond her media career, Winfrey has made significant contributions to education and social causes. She also founded OWN, the Oprah Winfrey Network.

Lesson: Oprah Winfrey's journey emphasizes the importance of resilience, self-belief, and using one's platform to make a positive impact.

Steve Jobs: The Creative Genius

Steve Jobs, co-founder of Apple Inc., is renowned for his innovative contributions to technology and design. Jobs' journey to success was not without its setbacks, but his unwavering commitment to excellence and creativity helped him achieve his goals.

Early Years: Jobs co-founded Apple with Steve Wozniak in 1976. The company's early success was marked by the introduction of the Apple II and the Macintosh.

Setbacks: Jobs faced a major setback in 1985 when he was ousted from Apple. Instead of giving up, he founded NeXT and acquired Pixar, which became a leader in computer animation.

Return to Apple: Jobs returned to Apple in 1997, leading the company to unprecedented success with the introduction of products like the iMac, iPod, iPhone, and iPad.

Legacy: Jobs' focus on innovation, design, and user experience transformed Apple into one of the most valuable companies in the world.

Lesson: Steve Jobs' story illustrates the power of innovation, perseverance, and a relentless pursuit of excellence.

Malala Yousafzai: The Courageous Advocate

Malala Yousafzai's journey from a young girl advocating for education in Pakistan to becoming the youngest Nobel Peace Prize laureate is a powerful example of courage and determination in achieving one's goals.

Early Advocacy: Malala began advocating for girls' education at a young age, writing a blog for the BBC under a pseudonym. Her activism brought her into conflict with the Taliban, who opposed girls' education.

Assassination Attempt: In 2012, Malala survived an assassination attempt by the Taliban, which brought global attention to her cause.

Global Impact: Malala continued her advocacy on a global scale, co-authoring the memoir "I Am Malala" and founding the Malala Fund to support education initiatives worldwide.

Nobel Peace Prize: In 2014, Malala was awarded the Nobel Peace Prize for her efforts to promote education and women's rights.

Lesson: Malala Yousafzai's journey highlights the power of courage, resilience, and unwavering commitment to a cause in achieving significant social change.

Jeff Bezos: The E-Commerce Pioneer

Jeff Bezos, the founder of Amazon, transformed an online bookstore into one of the world's largest and most influential companies. Bezos' strategic vision and relentless focus on customer satisfaction were key to his success.

Founding Amazon: Bezos founded Amazon in 1994 with the goal of creating an online marketplace for books. He started the company in his garage and focused on long-term growth rather than short-term profits.

Expansion: Under Bezos' leadership, Amazon expanded its product offerings, developed innovative services like Amazon Prime, and ventured into cloud computing with Amazon Web Services (AWS).

Customer-Centric Approach: Bezos' emphasis on customer satisfaction and innovation drove Amazon's success. His focus on data-driven decision-making and operational efficiency helped Amazon dominate the e-commerce market.

Blue Origin: In addition to Amazon, Bezos founded Blue Origin, a space exploration company, reflecting his long-term vision for space travel.

Lesson: Jeff Bezos' story underscores the importance of strategic vision, customer focus, and continuous innovation in achieving business success.

Conclusion: Learning from the Achievers

The stories of these famous individuals illustrate that achieving one's goals often involves overcoming significant challenges, embracing innovation, and maintaining a relentless focus on one's vision. Whether it's through resilience, creativity, strategic thinking, or advocacy, these achievers demonstrate that success is not a straight path but a journey marked by determination and perseverance. By learning from their experiences, we can gain valuable insights into the qualities and strategies that drive success, inspiring us to pursue our own goals with renewed vigor and confidence.

Chapter 4: Key Habits of Successful People

Success, in many ways, is the result of a series of consistent habits and behaviors. While talent and opportunity play a role, it is the daily habits that often distinguish the successful from the unsuccessful. This chapter delves into the key habits that successful people cultivate to achieve their goals and maintain their success.

Goal Setting and Planning

Habit: Successful people set clear, specific goals and develop detailed plans to achieve them. They break down long-term objectives into manageable short-term tasks.

Example: Bill Gates, co-founder of Microsoft, was known for his meticulous planning and goal-setting. From an early age, he had a clear vision for the personal computer revolution and set precise goals to make it a reality.

Practice:

- Write down your goals and break them into actionable steps.

- Review and adjust your plans regularly to stay on track.

Prioritizing and Time Management

Habit: Time is one of the most valuable resources. Successful individuals prioritize their tasks, focusing on what truly matters and avoiding distractions.

Example: Warren Buffett, one of the most successful investors, emphasizes the importance of saying "no" to almost everything to stay focused on his top priorities.

Practice:

- Use time management tools like calendars and to-do lists.

- Identify your most important tasks (MITs) and tackle them first.

Continuous Learning and Self-Improvement

Habit: Successful people are lifelong learners. They constantly seek new knowledge and skills to stay ahead in their fields.

Example: Oprah Winfrey is a voracious reader and a strong advocate for education and self-improvement. She often shares her learning experiences and insights with her audience.

Practice:

- Set aside time each day for reading and learning.

- Attend workshops, courses, and seminars to enhance your skills.

Maintaining a Healthy Lifestyle

Habit: Physical health is crucial for sustained success. Successful individuals prioritize exercise, nutrition, and adequate sleep.

Example: Richard Branson, founder of the Virgin Group, attributes his productivity and success to his active lifestyle, which includes regular exercise and outdoor activities.

Practice:

- Incorporate regular physical activity into your daily routine.

- Eat a balanced diet and ensure you get enough rest.

Building Strong Relationships

Habit: Networking and building meaningful relationships are key to success. Successful people invest time in creating and maintaining a strong network of contacts.

Example: Sheryl Sandberg, COO of Facebook, emphasizes the importance of mentorship and building supportive professional relationships.

Practice:

- Attend networking events and engage with others in your industry.

- Foster genuine connections by offering help and support.

Embracing Failure and Resilience

Habit: Successful individuals view failure as a learning opportunity. They are resilient and persist in the face of setbacks.

Example: Thomas Edison famously failed thousands of times before successfully inventing the light bulb. He saw each failure as a step closer to success.

Practice:

- Reflect on your failures and identify lessons learned.

- Develop a mindset that views challenges as opportunities for growth.

Practicing Gratitude and Positivity

Habit: Gratitude and a positive mindset are common traits among successful people. They focus on what they have rather than what they lack.

Example: Tony Robbins, a motivational speaker and life coach, incorporates gratitude practices into his daily routine to maintain a positive outlook.

Practice:

- Keep a gratitude journal and write down things you are thankful for each day.

- Surround yourself with positive influences and practice affirmations.

Effective Communication

Habit: Clear and effective communication is essential for leadership and collaboration. Successful people are adept at expressing their ideas and listening to others.

Example: Steve Jobs was known for his exceptional communication skills, which he used to inspire his team and convey his vision.

Practice:

- Work on your public speaking and presentation skills.

- Practice active listening and seek feedback to improve.

Taking Calculated Risks

Habit: Success often involves taking risks. However, successful individuals take calculated risks, weighing potential benefits against possible downsides.

Example: Elon Musk is known for taking bold risks with ventures like SpaceX and Tesla, which have revolutionized their respective industries.

Practice:

- Analyze the potential outcomes before making decisions.

- Be willing to step out of your comfort zone to seize opportunities.

Giving Back and Contributing to Society

Habit: Many successful people find fulfillment in giving back to their communities and contributing to causes they care about.

Example: Bill and Melinda Gates have dedicated a significant portion of their wealth to philanthropy through the Bill & Melinda Gates Foundation.

Practice:

- Volunteer your time and resources to charitable organizations.

- Find ways to make a positive impact in your community.

Conclusion: Cultivating Success Through Habits

The habits of successful people are not innate traits but learned behaviors that can be cultivated over time. By adopting these key habits—goal setting, prioritizing, continuous learning, maintaining health, building relationships, embracing failure, practicing gratitude, effective communication, taking risks, and giving back—you can set yourself on a path to achieving your goals and sustaining success. Remember, success is a journey, not a destination, and it is the consistent practice of these habits that will help you reach your full potential.

Continuous Learning Habits: Examples from Successful People

Continuous learning is a cornerstone of success, as it allows individuals to stay current, innovate, and adapt to changing circumstances. Here are some habits and practices of continuous learning exemplified by successful people:

Reading Regularly

Example: Warren Buffett

- Habit: Warren Buffett spends about 80% of his day reading. He recommends reading 500 pages a day to build knowledge, comparing it to compound interest.

- Practice: Set aside dedicated time each day for reading. Choose a mix of books, articles, and reports relevant to your field and interests.

Attending Workshops and Seminars

Example: Bill Gates

- Habit: Bill Gates frequently attends lectures, seminars, and events where he can learn from experts in various fields.

- Practice: Identify workshops and seminars in your area of interest. Attend these events to gain new insights and network with other professionals.

Taking Online Courses

Example: Sheryl Sandberg

- Habit: Sheryl Sandberg, COO of Facebook, has taken online courses to keep her skills sharp and learn about new trends and technologies.

- Practice: Enroll in online courses on platforms like Coursera, edX, or Udemy. Choose courses that align with your career goals and personal interests.

Seeking Mentorship

Example: Oprah Winfrey

- Habit: Oprah Winfrey attributes much of her success to the guidance she received from mentors. She actively seeks advice and learns from others' experiences.

- Practice: Find a mentor who can provide guidance and feedback. Regularly seek their advice and learn from their experiences and insights.

Participating in Professional Organizations

Example: Elon Musk

- Habit: Elon Musk participates in various professional organizations and forums where he can discuss ideas and learn from peers.

- Practice: Join professional organizations related to your industry. Attend their meetings, conferences, and networking events to stay informed and engaged.

Experimenting and Innovating

Example: Steve Jobs

- Habit: Steve Jobs was known for his relentless pursuit of innovation. He continuously experimented with new ideas and technologies.

- Practice: Create a habit of experimenting with new ideas and approaches. Don't be afraid to fail; use failures as learning experiences to refine your methods.

Keeping a Learning Journal

Example: Richard Branson

- Habit: Richard Branson keeps a notebook to jot down ideas, insights, and lessons learned. This helps him reflect on his experiences and continuously improve.

- Practice: Maintain a learning journal where you document what you learn each day. Reflect on these entries regularly to reinforce your learning.

Engaging in Peer Learning

Example: Jeff Bezos

- Habit: Jeff Bezos encourages peer learning within Amazon by promoting a culture of knowledge sharing and collaboration.

- Practice: Engage in peer learning by participating in study groups, discussion forums, or knowledge-sharing sessions with colleagues.

Setting Learning Goals

Example: Barack Obama

- Habit: Barack Obama sets specific learning goals for himself, whether it's reading a certain number of books or learning about a new topic.

- Practice: Set clear learning goals and track your progress. Whether it's mastering a new skill or gaining knowledge in a particular area, having defined objectives can keep you motivated.

Staying Curious and Asking Questions

Example: Albert Einstein

- Habit: Albert Einstein maintained a childlike curiosity throughout his life, always asking questions and seeking to understand the world better.

- Practice: Cultivate curiosity by asking questions and seeking answers. Approach problems with a curious mind and a desire to learn more.

Conclusion: Embracing Continuous Learning

Continuous learning is not just about acquiring new information but also about developing a mindset that values growth and improvement. By adopting these habits, you can create a lifelong learning routine that helps you stay ahead in your field and achieve your personal and professional goals. Whether it's reading regularly, attending courses, seeking mentorship, or simply staying curious, each of these practices contributes to a richer, more informed, and successful life.

Examples of Effective Time Management

Effective time management is crucial for achieving success in both personal and professional realms. It involves prioritizing tasks, avoiding distractions, and making the most of the time available. Here are some examples of how successful people manage their time effectively:

Prioritizing Tasks with the Eisenhower Matrix

Example: Dwight D. Eisenhower

- *Habit: The Eisenhower Matrix, also known as the Urgent-Important Matrix, was used by Dwight D. Eisenhower to prioritize his tasks. It involves categorizing tasks into four quadrants: urgent and important, important but not urgent, urgent but not important, and neither urgent nor important.*

- Practice: Create a matrix to categorize your tasks and focus on completing the urgent and important ones first. Delegate or postpone tasks that are not as critical.

Time Blocking

Example: Elon Musk

- *Habit: Elon Musk is known for his rigorous time-blocking method. He schedules his day in five-minute blocks, ensuring that each minute is accounted for and used productively.*

- Practice: Plan your day by blocking out specific times for different tasks and activities. Stick to your schedule to maximize productivity.

The Pomodoro Technique

Example: Francesco Cirillo (developer of the technique)

- Habit: The Pomodoro Technique involves working in focused intervals (usually 25 minutes) followed by a short break. This helps maintain high levels of concentration and prevents burnout.

- Practice: Use a timer to work in 25-minute intervals, taking a 5-minute break after each session. After four sessions, take a longer break (15-30 minutes).

Delegation

Example: Richard Branson

- Habit: Richard Branson emphasizes the importance of delegation. He trusts his team members with tasks that align with their strengths, freeing up his time to focus on strategic decisions.

- Practice: Identify tasks that can be delegated to others. Trust your team and provide them with the resources they need to succeed.

Setting SMART Goals

Example: Bill Gates

- Habit: Bill Gates sets SMART goals (Specific, Measurable, Achievable, Relevant, Time-bound) to ensure his objectives are clear and attainable within a certain timeframe.

- Practice: Define your goals using the SMART criteria. Break down larger goals into smaller, actionable steps and set deadlines for each.

Morning Routine

Example: Tim Cook

- Habit: Apple CEO Tim Cook starts his day early, often at 4:30 AM. He uses the quiet morning hours to exercise, read emails, and plan his day.

- Practice: Establish a morning routine that includes time for planning your day. Use this quiet time to focus on high-priority tasks without interruptions.

Eliminating Distractions

Example: Barack Obama

- Habit: Barack Obama minimizes decision fatigue by limiting his choices for daily routines, such as wearing only gray or blue suits. This helps him focus on more important decisions.

- Practice: Identify and eliminate distractions in your environment. Simplify routine tasks to reduce decision fatigue and stay focused on what matters.

Batch Processing

Example: Tim Ferriss

- Habit: Tim Ferriss, author of "The 4-Hour Workweek," advocates for batch processing similar tasks together to improve efficiency. For example, he processes all emails at specific times rather than continuously throughout the day.

- Practice: Group similar tasks and handle them in dedicated time blocks. This reduces the time lost in context-switching and improves overall efficiency.

Using Productivity Tools

Example: Sheryl Sandberg

- Habit: Sheryl Sandberg, COO of Facebook, utilizes various productivity tools to manage her tasks and time effectively. She relies on digital calendars, task management apps, and collaboration tools.

- Practice: Integrate productivity tools like Trello, Asana, or Microsoft To-Do into your workflow to keep track of tasks, set reminders, and collaborate with others.

Improving Your Time Blocking Technique

Time blocking is a powerful productivity technique that involves scheduling specific blocks of time for different tasks or activities throughout your day. This method helps you manage your time more efficiently, reduce distractions, and maintain focus. Here are some strategies to improve your time blocking:

Plan Ahead

Strategy: Dedicate time at the end of each day or week to plan your schedule for the following day or week.

Practice:

- Review your tasks and prioritize them based on importance and deadlines.

- Allocate specific time blocks for each task, considering the time you realistically need to complete them.

Use a Calendar

Strategy: Utilize a digital or physical calendar to organize your time blocks visually.

Practice:

- Use tools like Google Calendar, Microsoft Outlook, or a physical planner to map out your schedule.

- Color-code different types of activities (e.g., work, exercise, leisure) to easily distinguish between them.

Be Realistic with Your Time

Strategy: Estimate the time required for each task accurately and avoid overloading your schedule.

Practice:

- Break down larger tasks into smaller, more manageable chunks.

- Allocate extra time for unexpected interruptions or overruns.

Prioritize Your Tasks

Strategy: Identify your most important tasks (MITs) and schedule them during your peak productivity times.

Practice:

- Determine when you are most productive (e.g., morning, afternoon).

- Schedule your high-priority tasks during these peak times to maximize efficiency.

Include Breaks

Strategy: Incorporate regular breaks to rest and recharge, preventing burnout.

Practice:

- Follow techniques like the Pomodoro Technique (25 minutes of work followed by a 5-minute break).

- Schedule longer breaks for meals and relaxation throughout the day.

Minimize Distractions

Strategy: Create an environment conducive to focused work and minimize potential distractions.

Practice:

- Turn off notifications on your phone and computer during work blocks.

- Set boundaries with colleagues or family members to minimize interruptions.

Review and Adjust

Strategy: Regularly review your time blocks and adjust as needed based on what works and what doesn't.

Practice:

- At the end of each day or week, reflect on what you accomplished and what needs improvement.

- Adjust your time blocks for the next period based on these reflections.

Use Buffer Time

Strategy: Include buffer time between tasks to account for overruns and transitions.

Practice:

- Schedule 5-10 minutes between tasks to wrap up and prepare for the next activity.

- Use this time to handle quick tasks or relax briefly.

Stay Flexible

Strategy: Be prepared to adjust your schedule as needed. Flexibility is key to managing unexpected changes.

Practice:

- If a high-priority task arises, be willing to shift your time blocks to accommodate it.

- Keep a list of tasks that can be easily rescheduled if necessary.

Commit to the Process

Strategy: Consistency is crucial. Commit to the time blocking process and give it time to become a habit.

Practice:

- Stick to your schedule as closely as possible.

- Regularly evaluate your progress and make incremental improvements.

Sample Time Blocking Schedule

Morning:

- 7:00 AM - 8:00 AM: Exercise

- 8:00 AM - 8:30 AM: Breakfast and personal time

- 8:30 AM - 9:00 AM: Plan and review the day's tasks

- 9:00 AM - 11:00 AM: Focused work on high-priority tasks (MITs)

- 11:00 AM - 11:15 AM: Break

Midday:

- 11:15 AM - 1:00 PM: Continue focused work

- 1:00 PM - 2:00 PM: Lunch break

- 2:00 PM - 3:30 PM: Meetings and collaborative work

Afternoon:

- 3:30 PM - 3:45 PM: Break

- 3:45 PM - 5:00 PM: Work on secondary tasks

- 5:00 PM - 5:30 PM: Review and wrap up

Evening:

- 5:30 PM - 7:00 PM: Dinner and relaxation

- 7:00 PM - 8:00 PM: Personal projects or learning

- 8:00 PM - 9:00 PM: Relaxation and family time

- 9:00 PM - 10:00 PM: Prepare for the next day

Conclusion

Improving your time blocking technique involves careful planning, realistic scheduling, and regular review. By prioritizing tasks, minimizing distractions, and staying flexible, you can make the most of your time and enhance your productivity. Remember, consistency and commitment are key to making time blocking an effective habit.

Strategies for Overcoming Procrastination

Procrastination is a common challenge that can hinder productivity and progress. Overcoming procrastination involves understanding its root causes and implementing effective strategies to address them. Here are some proven strategies to help you overcome procrastination:

Break Tasks into Smaller Steps

Strategy: Large tasks can feel overwhelming, leading to procrastination. Breaking them into smaller, manageable steps makes them more approachable.

Practice:

- Identify the first small step you need to take to get started.

- Focus on completing one step at a time rather than the entire task.

Set Clear Goals and Deadlines

Strategy: Clear goals and deadlines provide structure and a sense of urgency.

Practice:

- Set specific, measurable, achievable, relevant, and time-bound (SMART) goals.

- Establish deadlines for each step of your task and stick to them.

Use Time Management Techniques

Strategy: Effective time management can reduce procrastination by organizing your tasks and time efficiently.

Practice:

- Apply the Pomodoro Technique (work for 25 minutes, then take a 5-minute break).

- Use time blocking to schedule dedicated time for each task.

Eliminate Distractions

Strategy: Identify and remove distractions from your environment to maintain focus.

Practice:

- Turn off notifications on your phone and computer.

- Create a dedicated workspace free from interruptions.

Prioritize Tasks

Strategy: Prioritizing tasks helps you focus on what's most important and prevents you from feeling overwhelmed.

Practice:

- Use the Eisenhower Matrix to categorize tasks by urgency and importance.

- Tackle high-priority tasks first.

Set a Timer for Short Bursts of Work

Strategy: Working in short, focused intervals can make tasks seem less daunting.

Practice:

- Set a timer for 10-15 minutes and work on a task until the timer goes off.

- Gradually increase the work intervals as you build momentum.

Develop a Routine

Strategy: Establishing a daily routine can create consistency and reduce procrastination.

Practice:

- Set specific times each day for work, breaks, and leisure activities.

- Stick to your routine to develop a habit of regular productivity.

Reward Yourself

Strategy: Rewards can provide motivation and positive reinforcement for completing tasks.

Practice:

- Set small rewards for completing individual tasks or steps.

- Treat yourself to a bigger reward after achieving major milestones.

Hold Yourself Accountable

Strategy: Accountability can keep you motivated and on track.

Practice:

- Share your goals and deadlines with a friend, family member, or colleague.

- Regularly update them on your progress and ask for their support.

Address Underlying Issues

Strategy: Procrastination can sometimes be a symptom of underlying issues such as fear of failure, perfectionism, or lack of motivation.

Practice:

- Reflect on why you might be procrastinating and address these underlying issues.

- Consider talking to a therapist or coach if procrastination is significantly impacting your life.

Visualize Success

Strategy: Visualizing the successful completion of a task can boost motivation and reduce procrastination.

Practice:

- Spend a few minutes each day visualizing yourself completing tasks and achieving your goals.

- Focus on the positive feelings and outcomes associated with success.

Change Your Environment

Strategy: Sometimes a change of environment can improve focus and reduce procrastination.

Practice:

- Find a quiet place to work, such as a library or a co-working space.

- Rearrange your workspace to create a more productive and inspiring environment.

Use Tools and Apps

Strategy: Productivity tools and apps can help you stay organized and focused.

Practice:

- Use apps like Trello, Asana, or Todoist to manage your tasks and deadlines.

- Use time-tracking apps to monitor how you spend your time.

Start with the Hardest Task

Strategy: Tackling the most difficult task first can give you a sense of accomplishment and make the rest of the day easier.

Practice:

- Identify your most challenging task and prioritize it in your schedule.

- Use the "Eat That Frog" technique, which involves completing the hardest task first thing in the morning.

Conclusion

Overcoming procrastination requires a combination of self-awareness, practical strategies, and consistent effort. By breaking tasks into smaller steps, setting clear goals, managing your time effectively, and eliminating distractions, you can reduce procrastination and enhance your productivity. Remember, the key is to start small and build momentum, gradually developing habits that support sustained progress and success.

Reflecting and Adjusting

Example: Benjamin Franklin

- Habit: Benjamin Franklin practiced daily reflection, assessing what went well and what could be improved. He adjusted his routines and strategies based on these reflections.

- Practice: Spend a few minutes at the end of each day reflecting on your accomplishments and challenges. Use these insights to adjust your approach and improve your time management.

Conclusion: Cultivating Effective Time Management Habits

Effective time management is about making conscious choices on how to spend your time to maximize productivity and achieve your goals. By adopting habits like prioritizing tasks, time blocking, using productivity techniques, and regularly reflecting on your progress, you can improve your efficiency and make the most of your time. Remember, successful people are not born with perfect time management skills—they develop them through consistent practice and continuous improvement.

Conclusion: Embrace the Journey to Success

As we wrap up this exploration of success, it's essential to remember that achieving your goals is a journey filled with challenges, learning, and growth. The habits, strategies, and examples we've discussed are tools to help you navigate this journey with confidence and resilience. Success is not just about reaching the destination but also about appreciating the progress and the lessons learned along the way.

In the next section, we will delve into a collection of inspiring quotes by famous individuals. These quotes are designed to motivate and uplift you, providing wisdom and encouragement for your personal and professional life. Whether you're seeking to inspire yourself, your colleagues, or your loved ones, these words of wisdom will offer valuable insights and perspectives.

Prepare to be inspired by the thoughts and reflections of some of the world's most successful and influential figures. These quotes will serve as a source of motivation, guiding you to stay focused, maintain a positive mindset, and persevere through any challenges you may face. Use these quotes to fuel your ambition and inspire those around you at work and at home.

Remember, success is a continuous journey, and with the right mindset and tools, you can achieve greatness. Stay inspired, stay motivated, and let these quotes be a beacon of light on your path to success.

Success Quotes by Famous People

"Success is not final failure is not fatal: It is the courage to continue that counts." – Winston Churchill

"Success usually comes to those who are too busy to be looking for it." – Henry David Thoreau

"Don't be afraid to give up the good to go for the great." – John D. Rockefeller

"I find that the harder I work the more luck I seem to have." – Thomas Jefferson

"Success is not the key to happiness. Happiness is the key to success. If you love what you are doing you will be successful." – Albert Schweitzer

"Success is walking from failure to failure with no loss of enthusiasm." – Winston Churchill

"The only place where success comes before work is in the dictionary." – Vidal Sassoon

"Success is how high you bounce when you hit bottom." – George S. Patton

"The road to success and the road to failure are almost exactly the same." – Colin R. Davis

"Opportunities don't happen. You create them." – Chris Grosser

"Don't be distracted by criticism. Remember—the only taste of success some people get is to take a bite out of you." – Zig Ziglar

"The way to get started is to quit talking and begin doing." – Walt Disney

"If you really look closely most overnight successes took a long time." – Steve Jobs

"The secret of success is to do the common thing uncommonly well." – John D. Rockefeller Jr.

"I never dreamed about success. I worked for it." – Estée Lauder

"Success seems to be connected with action. Successful people keep moving. They make mistakes but they don't quit." – Conrad Hilton

"There are no secrets to success. It is the result of preparation hard work and learning from failure." – Colin Powell

"The real test is not whether you avoid this failure because you won't. It's whether you let it harden or shame you into inaction or whether you learn from it; whether you choose to persevere." – Barack Obama

"The only limit to our realization of tomorrow will be our doubts of today." – Franklin D. Roosevelt

"Success is not in what you have but who you are." – Bo Bennett

"Success is getting what you want happiness is wanting what you get." – W. P. Kinsella

"Success isn't about how much money you make; it's about the difference you make in people's lives." – Michelle Obama

"Success is the sum of small efforts repeated day in and day out." – Robert Collier

"The biggest challenge after success is shutting up about it." – Criss Jami

"To succeed in life you need two things: ignorance and confidence." – Mark Twain

"Success is to be measured not so much by the position that one has reached in life as by the obstacles which he has overcome." – Booker T. Washington

"Success is not how high you have climbed but how you make a positive difference to the world." – Roy T. Bennett

"The difference between successful people and very successful people is that very successful people say 'no' to almost everything." – Warren Buffett

"Success is not the absence of failure; it's the persistence through failure." – Aisha Tyler

"Success is about creating benefit for all and enjoying the process. If you focus on this and adopt this definition success is yours." – Kelly Kim

"The key to success is to focus our conscious mind on things we desire not things we fear." – Brian Tracy

"There is no elevator to success you have to take the stairs." – Zig Ziglar

"Success is a state of mind. If you want success start thinking of yourself as a success." – Joyce Brothers

"Success is liking yourself liking what you do and liking how you do it." – Maya Angelou

"The true success is the person who invented himself." – Al Goldstein

"Success is doing ordinary things extraordinarily well." – Jim Rohn

"Action is the foundational key to all success." – Pablo Picasso

"Success is not measured by what you accomplish but by the opposition you have encountered and the courage with which you have maintained the struggle against overwhelming odds." – Orison Swett Marden

"Success is a journey not a destination. The doing is often more important than the outcome." – Arthur Ashe

"Success is the progressive realization of a worthy goal or ideal." – Earl Nightingale

"Success is falling nine times and getting up ten." – Jon Bon Jovi

"Success is achieved and maintained by those who try and keep trying." – W. Clement Stone

"The secret to success is to know something nobody else knows." – Aristotle Onassis

"Success is when preparation meets opportunity." – Bobby Unser

"Success is not just about making money. It's about making a difference." – Unknown

"Success consists of going from failure to failure without loss of enthusiasm." – Winston Churchill

"Success is not to be pursued; it is to be attracted by the person you become." – Jim Rohn

"Success is only meaningful and enjoyable if it feels like your own." – Michelle Obama

"Success is the sum of small efforts repeated day-in and day-out." – Robert Collier

"Success is not in never falling but in rising every time we fall." – Confucius

"The path to success is to take massive determined action." – Tony Robbins

"Success is finding satisfaction in giving a little more than you take." – Christopher Reeve

"Success is doing what you love and loving what you do." – Unknown

"Success is measured by the stories you can tell." – Unknown

"The only way to achieve the impossible is to believe it is possible." – Charles Kingsleigh

"Success is not the result of spontaneous combustion. You must set yourself on fire." – Arnold H. Glasow

"Success is simple. Do what's right the right way at the right time." – Arnold H. Glasow

"Success is a journey of persistence patience and personal growth." – Unknown

"Success is best when it's shared." – Howard Schultz

"Success is getting what you want. Happiness is wanting what you get." – Dale Carnegie

"Success is finding purpose in life and pursuing it with passion." – John C. Maxwell

"Success is a ladder you cannot climb with your hands in your pockets." – Mark Caine

"Success is not just a measure of how big you can DREAM it is also a measure of how much you can DO." – Stephen Richards

"Success is not built on success. It's built on failure. It's built on frustration. Sometimes it's built on catastrophe." – Sumner Redstone

"Success is no accident. It is hard work perseverance learning studying sacrifice and most of all love of what you are doing or learning to do." – Pelé

"Success means doing the best we can with what we have. Success is the doing not the getting; in the trying not the triumph. Success is a personal standard reaching for the highest that is in us becoming all that we can be." – Zig Ziglar

"Success is not how far you got but the distance you traveled from where you started." – Steve Prefontaine

"Success is sweet and sweeter if long delayed and gotten through many struggles and defeats." – Amos Bronson Alcott

"Success is nothing more than a few simple disciplines practiced every day." – Jim Rohn

"Success is not how high you have climbed but how you make a positive difference to the world." – Roy T. Bennett

"Success is nothing more than a few simple disciplines practiced every day." – Jim Rohn

"The way to get started is to quit talking and begin doing." – Walt Disney

"The road to success and the road to failure are almost exactly the same." – Colin R. Davis

"Successful people do what unsuccessful people are not willing to do. Don't wish it were easier; wish you were better." – Jim Rohn

"Stop chasing the money and start chasing the passion." – Tony Hsieh

"If you want to achieve greatness stop asking for permission." – Unknown

"Things work out best for those who make the best of how things work out." – John Wooden

"The successful warrior is the average man with laser-like focus." – Bruce Lee

"The road to success and the road to failure are almost exactly the same." – Colin R. Davis

"The only place where success comes before work is in the dictionary." – Vidal Sassoon

"The secret of success is to do the common thing uncommonly well." – John D. Rockefeller Jr.

"I never dreamed about success. I worked for it." – Estée Lauder

"Success is not in never falling but in rising every time we fall." – Confucius

"The difference between successful people and very successful people is that very successful people say 'no' to almost everything." – Warren Buffett

"Success is liking yourself liking what you do and liking how you do it." – Maya Angelou

"Success is walking from failure to failure with no loss of enthusiasm." – Winston Churchill

"Success is not built on success. It's built on failure. It's built on frustration. Sometimes it's built on catastrophe." – Sumner Redstone

"Success is going from failure to failure without losing your enthusiasm." – Winston Churchill

"Success is the result of preparation hard work and learning from failure." – Colin Powell

"The real test is not whether you avoid this failure because you won't. It's whether you let it harden or shame you into inaction or whether you learn from it; whether you choose to persevere." – Barack Obama

"Success is liking yourself liking what you do and liking how you do it." – Maya Angelou

"The successful warrior is the average man with laser-like focus." – Bruce Lee

"The only limit to our realization of tomorrow will be our doubts of today." – Franklin D. Roosevelt

"Winning isn't everything, it's the only thing." – Vince Lombardi

"The will to win is important, but the will to prepare is vital." – Joe Paterno

"Winning is a habit. Unfortunately, so is losing." – Vince Lombardi

"It's not whether you win or lose, it's how you play the game." – Grantland Rice

"Winners never quit and quitters never win." – Vince Lombardi

"Winning takes talent, to repeat takes character." – John Wooden

"Winning is fun, but those moments that you can touch someone's life in a very positive way are better." – Tim Howard

"Victory is sweetest when you've known defeat." – Malcolm S. Forbes

"The harder the battle, the sweeter the victory." – Les Brown

"To be prepared is half the victory." – Miguel de Cervantes

"It's not the will to win that matters—everyone has that. It's the will to prepare to win that matters." – Paul Bryant

"Winning isn't everything, but wanting to win is." – Arnold Palmer

"Sometimes you win, sometimes you learn." – John Maxwell

"Winning isn't getting ahead of others. It's getting ahead of yourself." – Roger Staubach

"You're never a loser until you quit trying." – Mike Ditka

"Winning is about having the whole team on the same page." – Bill Walton

"The secret of your future is hidden in your daily routine." – Mike Murdock

"There are no shortcuts to victory." – Matshona Dhliwayo

"Winning is not everything, but the effort to win is." Zig Ziglar

"Success is not the result of spontaneous combustion. You must set yourself on fire." – Arnold H. Glasow

"First they ignore you, then they laugh at you, then they fight you, then you win." – Mahatma Gandhi

"Winning doesn't always mean being first. Winning means you're doing better than you've ever done before." – Bonnie Blair

"You were born to win, but to be a winner, you must plan to win, prepare to win, and expect to win." – Zig Ziglar

"The difference between winning and losing is most often not quitting." – Walt Disney

"Winning isn't everything, but the will to win is everything." – Vince Lombardi

"The only way to prove that you're a good sport is to lose." – Ernie Banks

"You can't win unless you learn how to lose." – Kareem Abdul-Jabbar

"Winning is great, sure, but if you are really going to do something in life, the secret is learning how to lose." – Wilma Rudolph

 "There is no substitute for victory." – Douglas MacArthur

 "Winning isn't everything, it's the only thing." – Henry Russell "Red" Sanders

"Success is not in never failing, but rising every time you fall!" – Jonathan Taylor Thomas

"The key to winning is poise under stress." – Paul Brown

"Winning means you're willing to go longer, work harder, and give more than anyone else." – Vince Lombardi

"Winning is not everything, but making the effort to win is." – Vince Lombardi

"Sometimes you win, sometimes you learn." – John C. Maxwell

"You can't win unless you learn how to lose." – Kareem Abdul-Jabbar

"Winning is a state of mind that embraces everything you do." – Bryce Courtenay

"Winning doesn't always mean being first. Winning means you're doing better than you've ever done before." – Bonnie Blair

"The only place success comes before work is in the dictionary." – Vince Lombardi

"Winning is a habit. Unfortunately, so is losing." – Vince Lombardi

"Determination is the wake-up call to the human will." – Anthony Robbins

"The difference between the impossible and the possible lies in a man's determination." – Tommy Lasorda

"The price of success is hard work, dedication to the job at hand, and the determination that whether we win or lose, we have applied the best of ourselves to the task at hand." – Vince Lombardi

"Fall seven times, stand up eight." – Japanese Proverb

"Failure will never overtake me if my determination to succeed is strong enough." – Og Mandino

"You can have anything you want if you are willing to give up the belief that you can't have it." – Dr. Robert Anthony

"The only limit to our realization of tomorrow will be our doubts of today." – Franklin D. Roosevelt

"Success is not final, failure is not fatal: It is the courage to continue that counts." – Winston Churchill

"Perseverance is not a long race; it is many short races one after the other." – Walter Elliot

"The man who can drive himself further once the effort gets painful is the man who will win." – Roger Bannister

"Determination gives you the resolve to keep going in spite of the roadblocks that lay before you." – Denis Waitley

"The surest way not to fail is to determine to succeed." – Richard Brinsley Sheridan

"You are never too old to set another goal or to dream a new dream." – C.S. Lewis

"What you get by achieving your goals is not as important as what you become by achieving your goals." – Zig Ziglar

"Victory is always possible for the person who refuses to stop fighting." – Napoleon Hill

"It does not matter how slowly you go as long as you do not stop." – Confucius

"The future belongs to those who believe in the beauty of their dreams." – Eleanor Roosevelt

"Success is the result of perfection, hard work, learning from failure, loyalty, and persistence." – Colin Powell

"If you fell down yesterday, stand up today." – H.G. Wells

"When you come to the end of your rope, tie a knot and hang on." – Franklin D. Roosevelt

"The only thing that can stop you is the doubt that you carry in your mind." – Unknown

"You may have to fight a battle more than once to win it." – Margaret Thatcher

"Your dreams don't have an expiration date. Take a deep breath and try again." – KT Witten

"Determination is doing what needs to be done even when you don't feel like doing it." – Unknown

"With ordinary talent and extraordinary perseverance, all things are attainable." – Thomas Fowell Buxton

"It always seems impossible until it's done." – Nelson Mandela

"You cannot swim for new horizons until you have courage to lose sight of the shore." – William Faulkner

"Determination and perseverance move the world; thinking that others will do it for you is a sure way to fail." – Marva Collins

"To conquer frustration, one must remain intensely focused on the outcome, not the obstacles." – T.F. Hodge

"You just can't beat the person who never gives up." – Babe Ruth

"Believe in yourself and all that you are. Know that there is something inside you that is greater than any obstacle." – Christian D. Larson

"We will either find a way or make one." – Hannibal

"A river cuts through rock, not because of its power, but because of its persistence." – Jim Watkins

"Determination is the key to success." – Unknown

"Keep your eyes on the stars, and your feet on the ground." – Theodore Roosevelt

"Courage is not having the strength to go on; it is going on when you don't have the strength." – Theodore Roosevelt

"Success is not for the chosen few, but for the few who choose." – Unknown

"Great works are performed not by strength, but by perseverance." – Samuel Johnson

"You must knock the door will open. Ask and you shall receive." – Lailah Gifty Akita

"Don't watch the clock; do what it does. Keep going." – Sam Levenson

"Failure is simply the opportunity to begin again, this time more intelligently." – Henry Ford

"Success is not final, failure is not fatal: It is the courage to continue that counts." – Winston Churchill

"Our greatest glory is not in never failing, but in rising every time we fail." – Confucius

"Only those who dare to fail greatly can ever achieve greatly." – Robert F. Kennedy

"Failure is the condiment that gives success its flavor." – Truman Capote

"I have not failed. I've just found 10,000 ways that won't work." – Thomas Edison

"Do not be embarrassed by your failures, learn from them and start again." – Richard Branson

"The only real mistake is the one from which we learn nothing." – Henry Ford

"Failure is the key to success; each mistake teaches us something." – Morihei Ueshiba

"Every adversity, every failure, every heartache carries with it the seed of an equal or greater benefit." – Napoleon Hill

"Failure is not the opposite of success; it's part of success." – Arianna Huffington

"The greatest glory in living lies not in never falling, but in rising every time we fall." – Nelson Mandela

"Success is stumbling from failure to failure with no loss of enthusiasm." – Winston Churchill

"Failure is a detour, not a dead-end street." – Zig Ziglar

"It is impossible to live without failing at something unless you live so cautiously that you might as well not have lived at all, in which case you have failed by default." – J.K. Rowling

"You always pass failure on your way to success." –
Mickey Rooney

"There is no failure except in no longer trying." –
Elbert Hubbard

"A man may fail many times but he isn't a failure until
he begins to blame somebody else." – John
Burroughs

"The only limit to our realization of tomorrow will be
our doubts of today." – Franklin D. Roosevelt

"The greatest mistake you can make in life is to be
continually fearing you will make one." – Elbert
Hubbard

"Failure is success if we learn from it." – Malcolm
Forbes

"There are no secrets to success. It is the result of
preparation, hard work, and learning from failure." –
Colin Powell

"I can accept failure; everyone fails at something. But I can't accept not trying." – Michael Jordan

"Winners are not afraid of losing. But losers are. Failure is part of the process of success. People who avoid failure also avoid success." – Robert T. Kiyosaki

"The road to success and the road to failure are almost exactly the same." – Colin R. Davis

"Failure should be our teacher, not our undertaker. Failure is delay, not defeat. It is a temporary detour, not a dead end." – Denis Waitley

"I have learned more from my failures than from my successes." – Humble The Poet

"The only way to avoid failure is to never try anything new." – Unknown

"The only real failure in life is not to be true to the best one knows." – Buddha

"It's fine to celebrate success, but it is more important to heed the lessons of failure." – Bill Gates

"Failure after long perseverance is much grander than never to have a striving good enough to be called a failure." – George Eliot

"The season of failure is the best time for sowing the seeds of success." – Paramahansa Yogananda

"Failure is only the opportunity to begin again, only this time more wisely." – Henry Ford

"Do not fear mistakes. You will know failure. Continue to reach out." – Benjamin Franklin

"Every failure is a step to success." – William Whewell

"Failure is a bruise, not a tattoo." – Jon Sinclair

"I'd rather be a failure at something I love than a success at something I hate." – George Burns

"Success depends on your backbone, not your wishbone." – Unknown

"Most great people have attained their greatest success just one step beyond their greatest failure." – Napoleon Hill

"Failure is a stepping stone to greatness." – Oprah Winfrey

"There are no secrets to success. It is the result of preparation, hard work, and learning from failure." – Colin Powell

"The only place where success comes before work is in the dictionary." – Vidal Sassoon

"The harder I work, the luckier I get." – Samuel Goldwyn

"Success is no accident. It is hard work, perseverance, learning, studying, sacrifice, and most of all, love of what you are doing or learning to do." – Pelé

"There is no substitute for hard work." – Thomas Edison

"Hard work beats talent when talent doesn't work hard." – Tim Notke

"The price of success is hard work, dedication to the job at hand, and the determination that whether we win or lose, we have applied the best of ourselves to the task at hand." – Vince Lombardi

"Dreams don't work unless you do." – John C. Maxwell

"I'm a greater believer in luck, and I find the harder I work, the more I have of it." – Thomas Jefferson

"Without hard work, nothing grows but weeds." – Gordon B. Hinckley

"Opportunities are usually disguised as hard work, so most people don't recognize them." – Ann Landers

"Success is the result of perfection, hard work, learning from failure, loyalty, and persistence." – Colin Powell

"Hard work spotlights the character of people: Some turn up their sleeves, some turn up their noses, and some don't turn up at all." – Sam Ewing

"Striving for success without hard work is like trying to harvest where you haven't planted." – David Bly

"There is no elevator to success; you have to take the stairs." – Zig Ziglar

"Good things come to those who work their asses off and never give up." – Unknown

"Success is the sum of small efforts, repeated day in and day out." – Robert Collier

"Perseverance is the hard work you do after you get tired of doing the hard work you already did." – Newt Gingrich

"The only way to achieve the impossible is to believe it is possible." – Charles Kingsleigh

"I'm a greater believer in luck, and I find the harder I work, the more I have of it." – Thomas Jefferson

"Great things come from hard work and perseverance. No excuses." – Kobe Bryant

"Work hard in silence, let your success be your noise." – Frank Ocean

"Hard work without talent is a shame, but talent without hard work is a tragedy." – Robert Half

"The difference between the impossible and the possible lies in a person's determination." – Tommy Lasorda

"Do not whine… Do not complain. Work harder. Spend more time alone." – Joan Didion

"The only place success comes before work is in the dictionary." – Vidal Sassoon

"The best way to not feel hopeless is to get up and do something. Don't wait for good things to happen to you. If you go out and make some good things happen, you will fill the world with hope, you will fill yourself with hope." – Barack Obama

"Hard work compounds like interest, and the earlier you do it, the more time you have for the benefits to pay off." – Sam Altman

"There is no magic to achievement. It's really about hard work, choices, and persistence." – Michelle Obama

"A dream does not become reality through magic; it takes sweat, determination, and hard work." – Colin Powell

"Work hard, be kind, and amazing things will happen." – Conan O'Brien

"There are no shortcuts to any place worth going." – Beverly Sills

"Success is not the result of spontaneous combustion. You must set yourself on fire." – Arnold H. Glasow

"The road to success is not easy to navigate, but with hard work, drive, and passion, it's possible to achieve the American dream." – Tommy Hilfiger

"Plans are only good intentions unless they immediately degenerate into hard work." – Peter Drucker

"I never dreamed about success. I worked for it." – Estée Lauder

"Hard work keeps the wrinkles out of the mind and spirit." – Helena Rubinstein

"You can't have a million-dollar dream with a minimum-wage work ethic." – Stephen C. Hogan

"Inspiration is the windfall from hard work and focus. Muses are too unreliable to keep on the payroll." – Helen Hanson

"Talent is cheaper than table salt. What separates the talented individual from the successful one is a lot of hard work." – Stephen King

"Talent is God-given. Be humble. Fame is man-given. Be grateful. Conceit is self-given. Be careful." – John Wooden

"Hard work beats talent when talent doesn't work hard." – Tim Notke

"Talent wins games, but teamwork and intelligence win championships." – Michael Jordan

"Use what talents you possess; the woods would be very silent if no birds sang there except those that sang best." – Henry Van Dyke

"Talent is cheaper than table salt. What separates the talented individual from the successful one is a lot of hard work." – Stephen King

"Everyone has talent. What is rare is the courage to follow the talent to the dark place where it leads." – Erica Jong

"Nothing in this world can take the place of persistence. Talent will not: nothing is more common than unsuccessful men with talent." – Calvin Coolidge

"Talent is a pursued interest. Anything that you're willing to practice, you can do." – Bob Ross

"Your talent is God's gift to you. What you do with it is your gift back to God." – Leo Buscaglia

"Talent does what it can; genius does what it must." –
Edward G. Bulwer-Lytton

"The most valuable thing you can make is a mistake –
you can't learn anything from being perfect." – Adam
Osborne

"Hide not your talents, they for use were made.
What's a sundial in the shade?" – Benjamin Franklin

"Talent without discipline is like an octopus on roller
skates. There's plenty of movement, but you never
know if it's going to be forward, backwards, or
sideways." – H. Jackson Brown Jr.

"We are told that talent creates its own opportunities.
But it sometimes seems that intense desire creates not
only its own opportunities but its own talents." – Eric
Hoffer

"A great deal of talent is lost to the world for want of
a little courage." – Sydney Smith

"There is no such thing as a great talent without great willpower." – Honore de Balzac

"Doing easily what others find difficult is talent; doing what is impossible for talent is genius." – Henri Frederic Amiel

"If you have talent, use it in every which way possible. Don't hoard it. Don't dole it out like a miser. Spend it lavishly like a millionaire intent on going broke." – Brendan Francis

"Talent hits a target no one else can hit; Genius hits a target no one else can see." – Arthur Schopenhauer

"The best way to get approval is not to need it." – Hugh MacLeod

"Genius is talent set on fire by courage." – Henry Van Dyke

"Talent develops in quiet places, character in the full current of human life." – Johann Wolfgang von Goethe

"Talent is nothing but a prolonged period of attention and a shortened period of mental assimilation." – Constantin Stanislavski

"Everyone has talent. What's rare is the courage to follow it to the dark places where it leads." – Erica Jong

"The artist is nothing without the gift, but the gift is nothing without work." – Emile Zola

"I believe that every person is born with talent." – Maya Angelou

"To understand one's destiny it is necessary to meet one's talent." – Walter Benjamin

"Talent alone won't make you a success. Neither will being in the right place at the right time, unless you are ready." – Johnny Carson

"The person born with a talent they are meant to use will find their greatest happiness in using it." – Johann Wolfgang von Goethe

"I have no special talent. I am only passionately curious." – Albert Einstein

"Work while you have the light. You are responsible for the talent that has been entrusted to you." – Henri Frederic Amiel

"To do what you love and feel that it matters how could anything be more fun?" – Katharine Graham

"Talent is the multiplier. The more energy and attention you invest in it, the greater the yield." – Marcus Buckingham

"Talent is the presence of ability and absence of understanding about the source and operation of that ability." – Joseph Chilton Pearce

"Talent is like electricity. We don't understand electricity. We use it." – Maya Angelou

"A really great talent finds its happiness in execution." – Johann Wolfgang von Goethe

"Use your talents. They are precious gifts given to you to put to work." – Rob Liano

"Hard work without talent is a shame, but talent without hard work is a tragedy." – Robert Half

"Talents are best nurtured in solitude; character is best formed in the stormy billows of the world." – Johann Wolfgang von Goethe

"To practice any art, no matter how well or badly, is a way to make your soul grow. So do it." – Kurt Vonnegut